THE CHRISTMAS EVENT

THE CHRISTMAS EVENT

WHAT'S IT ALL ABOUT?

IVAN MOORHOUSE

The Christmas Event

Copyright © 2019 by Ivan Moorhouse. All rights reserved.

No part of this publication may be reproduced, stored in a retrieval system or transmitted in any way by any means, electronic, mechanical, photocopy, recording or otherwise without the prior permission of the author except as provided by USA copyright law.

The opinions expressed by the author are not necessarily those of URLink Print and Media.

1603 Capitol Ave., Suite 310 Cheyenne, Wyoming USA 82001
1-888-980-6523 | admin@urlinkpublishing.com

URLink Print and Media is committed to excellence in the publishing industry.

Book design copyright © 2018 by URLink Print and Media. All rights reserved.

Published in the United States of America

ISBN 978-1-64367-262-5 (Paperback)
ISBN 978-1-64367-261-8 (Digital)

Non-Fiction
13.02.19

CONTENTS

Introduction 7
Chapter 1:   The Gospel Account 9
Chapter 2:   The Historical And Biblical
             Background To Christmas 17
Post Script: Some Questions To Ponder 32
Chapter 3:   What Christmas Means To Me and
             How We Celebrate It: The Testimonies
             of People Around the World....................34
Bibliography..43
Appendix: Old Testament Prophecies Specifically About
             The Birth and Infant Years of Christ..........45

INTRODUCTION

Christmas is generally a time of holiday, celebration, merry-making, friendly greetings (such as Christmas cards) and gift giving around the world, particularly in western countries where Christianity has had most influence. For a number of reasons, light is a prominent feature, hence the preponderance of Christmas lights in and around homes, streets and shopping malls. Now that we live in a 'global village', the event with all its trimmings is purveyed all around the world by means of the internet, television, radio and social media.

The name *Christmas* denotes the celebration of the coming of the Christ or Messiah into the world as recorded in the Bible. This is presented in sequential order in chapter one. In the modern world the spiritual celebration has been somewhat superseded by more secular celebrations. This is, however, not something entirely new – the same was true centuries ago. For those who are Christian in belief attendance at events such as carol singing and worship services is normal practice. This varies in flavour throughout the world as is described by people of different nationalities in chapter three. Nevertheless, even amongst Christians, Christmas can be a controversial topic since its origins, while certainly religious, are not particular Christian, as is explained in chapter two.

This little book aims to explore the origins of the Christmas event and present a brief history of the celebration. It simply serves to provide an explanation to those who wish to know a little more of what it's all about.

CHAPTER 1

THE GOSPEL ACCOUNT

Events leading up to Christ's birth

The Birth of Jesus Foretold

In the sixth month of Elizabeth's pregnancy[1], God sent the angel Gabriel to Nazareth, a town in Galilee, to a virgin pledged to be married to a man named Joseph, a descendant of David. The virgin's name was Mary. The angel went to her and said, "Greetings, you who are highly favoured! The Lord is with you."

Mary was greatly troubled at his words and wondered what kind of greeting this might be. But the angel said to her, "Do not be afraid, Mary; you have found favour with God. You will conceive and give birth to a son, and you are to call him Jesus. He will be great and will be called the Son of the Most High. The Lord God will give him the throne of his father David, and he will reign over Jacob's descendants forever; his kingdom will never end."

"How will this be," Mary asked the angel, "since I am a virgin?"

The angel answered, "The Holy Spirit will come on you, and the power of the Most High will overshadow you. So the holy one to be born will be called the Son of God. Even Elizabeth your relative

---

[1] Elizabeth, Mary's cousin, was expecting a son who was to become John the Baptist.

is going to have a child in her old age, and she who was said to be unable to conceive is in her sixth month. For no word from God will ever fail."

"I am the Lord's servant," Mary answered. "May your word to me be fulfilled." Then the angel left her.

Mary Visits Elizabeth

At that time Mary got ready and hurried to a town in the hill country of Judea, where she entered Zechariah's home and greeted Elizabeth. When Elizabeth heard Mary's greeting, the baby leaped in her womb, and Elizabeth was filled with the Holy Spirit. In a loud voice she exclaimed: "Blessed are you among women, and blessed is the child you will bear! But why am I so favoured, that the mother of my Lord should come to me? As soon as the sound of your greeting reached my ears, the baby in my womb leaped for joy. Blessed is she who has believed that the Lord would fulfil his promises to her!"

And Mary said:

> "My soul glorifies the Lord and my spirit rejoices in God my Saviour, for he has been mindful of the humble state of his servant.
>
> From now on all generations will call me blessed, for the Mighty One has done great things for me— holy is his name.
>
> His mercy extends to those who fear him, from generation to generation.
>
> He has performed mighty deeds with his arm; he has scattered those who are proud in their inmost thoughts.
>
> He has brought down rulers from their thrones but has lifted up the humble.
>
> He has filled the hungry with good things but has sent the rich away empty.

He has helped his servant Israel, remembering to be
merciful to Abraham and his descendants forever, just
as he promised our ancestors."

Mary stayed with Elizabeth for about three months and then returned home.

Excerpted from the Gospel of Luke Chapter 1, verses 26-56.

The Birth of Jesus

This is how the birth of Jesus Christ came about: His mother Mary was pledged to be married to Joseph, but before they came together, she was found to be with child through the Holy Spirit.

Because Joseph her husband was a righteous man and did not want to expose her to public disgrace, he had in mind to divorce her quietly. But after he had considered this, an angel of the Lord appeared to him in a dream and said, "Joseph son of David, do not be afraid to take Mary home as your wife, because what is conceived in her is from the Holy Spirit. She will give birth to a son, and you are to give him the name Jesus, because he will save his people from their sins".

All this took place to fulfil what the Lord had said through the prophet:

> The virgin will be with child and will give birth to a
> son, and they will call him Immanuel–which means,
> God with us[2].

When Joseph woke up, he did what the angel of the Lord had commanded him and took Mary home as his wife. But he had no union with her until she gave birth to a son.

---

[2] Isaiah 7:14

In those days Caesar Augustus issued a decree that a census should be taken of the entire Roman world. (This was the first census that took place while Quirinius was governor of Syria.) And everyone went to his own town to register. So Joseph also went up from the town of Nazareth in Galilee to Judea, to Bethlehem the town of David, because he belonged to the house and line of David. He went there to register with Mary, who was pledged to be married to him and was expecting a child.

While they were there, the time came for the baby to be born, and she gave birth to her firstborn, a son. She wrapped him in cloths and placed him in a manger, because there was no room for them in the inn.

And there were shepherds living out in the fields nearby, keeping watch over their flocks at night. An angel of the Lord appeared to them, and the glory of the Lord shone around them, and they were terrified. But the angel said to them,

> "Do not be afraid. I bring you good news of great joy that will be for all the people. Today in the town of David a Saviour has been born to you; he is Christ the Lord. This will be a sign to you: You will find a baby wrapped in cloths and lying in a manger".

Suddenly a great company of the heavenly host appeared with the angel, praising God and saying,

> "Glory to God in the highest, and on earth peace to men on whom his favour rests".

When the angels had left them and gone into heaven, the shepherds said to one another, "Let's go to Bethlehem and see this thing that has happened, which the Lord has told us about". So they hurried off and found Mary and Joseph, and the baby, who was lying in the manger.

When they had seen him, the shepherds returned, glorifying and praising God, and they spread the word concerning what had been told them about this child, and all who heard it were amazed at what the shepherds said to them. But Mary treasured up all these things and pondered them in her heart.

> *Excerpted from the Gospels of Matthew (Chapter 1:18-25) and Luke (Chapter 2:1-20).*

Events following the birth of Christ

Jesus Presented in the Temple

On the eighth day, when it was time to circumcise him, he was named Jesus, the name the angel had given him before he had been conceived. When the time of their purification according to the Law of Moses had been completed[3], Joseph and Mary took him to Jerusalem to present him to the Lord (as it is written in the Law of the Lord, 'Every firstborn male is to be consecrated to the Lord'[4]), and to offer a sacrifice in keeping with what is said in the Law of the Lord: a pair of doves or two young pigeons[5].

Now there was a man in Jerusalem called Simeon, who was righteous and devout. He was waiting for the consolation of Israel, and the Holy Spirit was upon him. It had been revealed to him by the Holy Spirit that he would not die before he had seen the Lord's Christ. Moved by the Spirit, he went into the temple courts. When the parents brought in the child Jesus to do for him what the custom of the Law required, Simeon took him in his arms and praised God, saying:

> "Sovereign Lord, as you have promised, you now dismiss your servant in peace. For my eyes have seen your salvation, which you have prepared in the sight of all people, a light for revelation to the Gentiles and for glory to your people Israel".

---

[3] See Leviticus 12:1-4
[4] Exodus 13:2,12
[5] Leviticus 12:8

The child's father and mother marvelled at what was said about him.

Then Simeon blessed them and said to Mary, his mother:

> "This child is destined to cause the falling and rising of many in Israel, and to be a sign that will be spoken against, so that the thoughts of many hearts will be revealed. And a sword will pierce your own soul too".

There was also a prophetess, Anna, the daughter of Phanuel, of the tribe of Asher. She was very old; she had lived with her husband seven years after her marriage, and then was a widow until she was eighty-four. She never left the temple but worshipped night and day, fasting and praying. Coming up to them at that very moment, she gave thanks to God and spoke about the child to all who were looking forward to the redemption of Jerusalem.

The Magi Visit the Messiah

After Jesus was born in Bethlehem in Judea, during the time of King Herod, Magi[6] from the east came to Jerusalem and asked,

> "Where is the one who has been born king of the Jews? We saw his star when it rose and have come to worship him."

When King Herod heard this he was disturbed, and all Jerusalem with him. When he had called together all the people's chief priests and teachers of the law, he asked them where the Messiah was to be born. "In Bethlehem in Judea," they replied, "for this is what the prophet has written:

> 'But you, Bethlehem, in the land of Judah, are by no means least among the rulers of Judah; for out of

---

[6] Traditionally wise men

you will come a ruler who will shepherd my people Israel.'"[7]

Then Herod called the Magi secretly and found out from them the exact time the star had appeared. He sent them to Bethlehem and said, "Go and search carefully for the child. As soon as you find him, report to me, so that I too may go and worship him."

After they had heard the king, they went on their way, and the star they had seen when it rose went ahead of them until it stopped over the place where the child was. When they saw the star, they were overjoyed. On coming to the house, they saw the child with his mother Mary, and they bowed down and worshiped him. Then they opened their treasures and presented him with gifts of gold, frankincense and myrrh. And having been warned in a dream not to go back to Herod, they returned to their country by another route.

The Escape to Egypt

When they had gone, an angel of the Lord appeared to Joseph in a dream. "Get up," he said, "take the child and his mother and escape to Egypt. Stay there until I tell you, for Herod is going to search for the child to kill him."

So he got up, took the child and his mother during the night and left for Egypt, where he stayed until the death of Herod. And so was fulfilled what the Lord had said through the prophet:

"Out of Egypt I called my son."[8]

When Herod realized that he had been outwitted by the Magi, he was furious, and he gave orders to kill all the boys in Bethlehem and its vicinity who were two years old and under, in accordance with the time he had learned from the Magi. Then what was said through the prophet Jeremiah was fulfilled:

---

[7] Micah 5:2,4
[8] Hosea 11:1

"A voice is heard in Ramah, weeping and great mourning, Rachel weeping for her children and refusing to be comforted, because they are no more."[9]

The Return to Nazareth

After Herod died, an angel of the Lord appeared in a dream to Joseph in Egypt and said, "Get up, take the child and his mother and go to the land of Israel, for those who were trying to take the child's life are dead."

So he got up, took the child and his mother and went to the land of Israel. But when he heard that Archelaus was reigning in Judea in place of his father Herod, he was afraid to go there. Having been warned in a dream, he withdrew to the district of Galilee, and he went and lived in a town called Nazareth. So was fulfilled what was said through the prophets, that he would be called a Nazarene[10].

Joseph and Mary had done everything required by the Law of the Lord. And the child grew and became strong; he was filled with wisdom, and the grace of God was upon him.

Excerpted from the Gospels of Matthew (Chapter 2:1-23) and Luke (Chapter 2: 21-40).

---

[9] Jeremiah 31:15

[10] This is not a prophecy recorded in the Old Testament but probably a fulfilment of Jewish anticipation of a humble and rejected Messiah (c/f Psalm 22, Isaiah 11:1, 53; Zechariah 11:4-14). Nazareth was an insignificant town viewed with contempt by many (see, for example, John 1:46).

CHAPTER 2

THE HISTORICAL AND BIBLICAL BACKGROUND TO CHRISTMAS

Christmas is a Christian festival celebrated worldwide. For those in the western world, as well as parts of the Developing World, Christmas has become probably the most materialistic, even hedonistic, of all the so-called ecclesiastical or church celebrations. The whole reason for the celebration, at least for Christians, is the birth of Jesus Christ in Bethlehem around 2000 years ago. However, the origin of this celebration is both interesting and contentious: extremely meaningful to some people and an anathema to others, depending where on the religious spectrum they are.

The Origins of the Actual Celebratory Event

Most people celebrate birthdays. Birthdays are times when we honor a person for who they are and mark another year in his or her life. Most people have records of their birthday (birth certificate, newspaper entry, baptismal certificate, etc.) and therefore will have been able to celebrate it from early childhood. Some famous people are often given mention over the media on their birthdays, for example the Queen of England. Not so with Jesus of Nazareth. We actually do not know on which day he was born; the Bible gives no indication of the date and it is certainly very unlikely to have been 25 December. All branches of the church agree that no data exists for determining the day, month or year of the event and such a festival was certainly not celebrated in Apostolic or early post-Apostolic times. In fact, the birth of Christ was probably only celebrated by the church for the first time in the middle of the third century.

So how has this event become so central to the calendar and important to large sections of the established church?

The first dated celebrations

Birthdays were not generally celebrated by Semitic people. The practice was rather an Aryan custom – the Persians, Greeks and Romans celebrated such days. Theologians and historians write off early Christian attempts to determine a date for the birth of Jesus as speculation and irrelevant. The theologian and New Testament scholar, Oscar Cullmann, described it as "all sorts of arithmetical and imaginative ingenuity"[11]. Some early Christian writers put the day in March or April for reasons associated with the March equinox, springtime and the importance of light and darkness (Jesus being described in Malachi 4:2 as the 'sun of righteousness'). However, it is pertinent to note here that some early Christian leaders such as Clement of Alexandria, Origen and Arnobius criticized, and indeed ridiculed, all attempts to arrive at such a date. Such deliberations were seen to be pagan since according to the biblical record only the heathen and godless like Pharaoh and Herod celebrated their birthdays. The primitive Christian church was more interested in the death and resurrection of Christ than his birthday and festivals in honour of Christian apostles and martyrs were associated with their deaths, not their birthdays.

The first date that enjoyed any acceptance in the early Christian church was January 6th. At least two streams of belief originally contributed to such a dating. Firstly, a dominant philosophy or doctrine in Greek thought was that of Gnosticism (= knowledge),

---

[11] Cullman, 1956.

a branch of which, *Docetism*, believed that Jesus was only divine between his baptism and his death. The great early Christian leader, Clement of Alexandria, tells us of a second century gnostic mystic from Alexandria in Egypt called Basilides who, together with his followers, celebrated the baptism of Jesus on either January 6th or 10th, believing that the *divine* Christ only appeared at his baptism where he received the affirmation of the Father God (Matt. 3:17). The Greek word for "appearing" is *epiphaneia* from which we get the word Epiphany, a festival celebrating the baptism of Jesus by the early church and still celebrated today by certain church traditions though with a different emphasis (addressed below).

In the pagan world of the first and second centuries, the feast of Dionysus, associated with the lengthening of days and increase in light following the northern hemispheric winter solstice on December 21st or 22nd, was celebrated on January 6th. In Alexandria, the birth of the divine Aeon (= 'eternal') was commemorated on that day, and on the night before January 6th the waters of the Nile were said to have had miraculous powers. Hence the Basilidean sect's practice of celebrating the water baptism of Jesus on that day. This festival was adopted by the Eastern Orthodox Church.

The Christian Church was nevertheless more interested in the birth of Jesus than his baptism since this was the time believed to be his appearing as the Divine One. What eventually happened, therefore, was that the two events were rolled into one continuous celebration: the night of January 5th was devoted to the festival of Christ's birth and the next day was devoted to a celebration of his baptism. This was also associated with the manifestation of the star from the east which announced Christ's appearance. According to Cullmann, this was the situation at the beginning of the fourth century onwards when the festival of Epiphany was celebrated with great splendour in Egypt, Syria and Palestine.

But what about December 25th, the current date of the celebration?

The Festival of December 25th

The origins of the Christmas event are generally agreed to be inherited from the Roman festival of *Saturnalia*, a celebration in honour of Saturn coinciding with the close of the vintage and harvest in December. This was a weeklong celebration which started on December 17th and usually ended with the feast of *Brumalia* – the birthday or rebirth of the sun – to coincide with the winter solstice. Lighted candles adorned the celebration symbolizing the search for truth and light.

In the pagan world of the second and third centuries, December 25th was observed as an important festival in honour of the sun god, a cult known as *Mithraism*. The Romans adopted the worship of the Mithraic sun god, whose birthday was celebrated on December 25th, from the conquered Persians. In 274 A.D., the Emperor Aureian made *sol invictus* (the invincible sun) the imperial religion and instituted the feast of *Dies Natalis Solis Invincti* – the Day of the Unconquerable Sun – on December 25th. The reason the chief festival was held on this date was because this was erroneously believed to be the date of the winter solstice in the northern hemisphere and thus an appropriate time to celebrate the reality of the sun and light. With the days beginning to lengthen and solar energy increasing, it was regarded as the birthday of the sun. Great bonfires were lit on that day and the 'unconquered sun' was worshipped.

The great emperor Constantine (c275-337) is described as the first emperor of Rome to become a Christian (he was baptized as a Christian on his deathbed). Under his reign Christians regained freedom of worship and the church became legal. However, he still promoted worship of the sun. It was Constantine who instituted the Christian "Lord's day" as an official day of rest – hence the name *Sunday*. It is thus probable that through his influence the festival of Christ's birth was changed from January 6th to December 25th. His intention to introduce a Christian form of pagan sun worship was consequently extended to the celebration of the birth of Christ.

The first authentic record of December 25th as the "Festival of the Nativity" is found in a Roman Church calendar compiled in 353-

354 and is part of a date list of pagan festivals probably first written in 336.

Thus far we can see that the celebration of what we call Christmas today had, in its embryonic form, a mixture of associated events drawn from both pagan and Christian beliefs, and while it does not always sit comfortably with many Christians, the fact remains that we have certain events in our Christian calendar which amount to 'Christianized other' celebrations, that is, non-Christian festivals which have been adopted by the church and given a distinctly Christian stamp.

It also needs to be said here that if shepherds were in the fields by night at the time of Christ's birth as recorded in the Gospel (Luke 2:8ff), it is unlikely to have been in December since it is too cold and wet to be outside with sheep at that time of year. This practice would only occur between April and September and therefore renders the December 25th date as improbable.

It is therefore clear that in terms of the origin and development of the celebration in Christian history, we are actually dealing with what is commonly known as *syncretism* which may be defined as the fusion or 'mixing' of religions whereby one or more lose their basic structure or identity. This will be dealt with in more detail under *Some theological reflections* below.

If we look at the signs of the festivals which were 'adapted' to fit the Christian celebration of the nativity, we see similarities such as sun and light being synonymous with the Son of God. For example, compare Malachi 4:2: '...the sun of righteousness will rise...' and John 8:12 where Jesus proclaims he is the light of the world.

Then there is the whole aspect of the appearing of the new sun year and the divine attributes of *Saturnalia* as seen against the appearing of the Son of God who birthed a new era and kingdom. And we cannot ignore the significance of the star of Bethlehem and it's association with the sun and light.

It's therefore clear that existing signs and codes were adopted by Christians, both under authority (Constantine) and choice. In the latter case, the examples of the great St. Augustine (4th to 5th centuries) and Pope Leo (early 16th century) can be cited. Both decried the pagan worship of the sun and encouraged Christian disciples to rather worship the Christ who, in Augustine's words, is "our *new sun*"[12]. Syncretism is common in all parts of the world to this day as various cultures encounter Christianity and vice versa.

The spread of the December 25th festival

The acceptance of the idea to separate the nativity festival from Epiphany outside of Rome was slow. We can track the spread of the festival eastward and southwards through the Christian church: first to one of the most important Christian centres, Antioch in Syria, in 375-6, then to Constantinople (Istanbul) in 378-81, Cappadocia (also in modern day Turkey) by 383 and Egypt in 431. Acceptance by the Jerusalem church took somewhat longer. It was probably not until the middle of the sixth century that the Palestinian Christians began celebrating the Holy Nativity on 25th December. Armenians, however, still celebrate Christmas on January 6th.

Once the Christian church of the first few centuries had universally accepted the December 25th festival, the date was firmly established for the rest of the world as the Christian message was carried on the back of civilisation around the globe over time.

The Feast of Epiphany celebrated on January 6th is still a very important event in the calendars of many Christian churches, particularly those of the sacramental tradition such as the Roman Catholic and Greek Orthodox traditions. It commemorates the appearing of Christ to the world and especially to the Gentiles since the wise men from the east arrived sometime *after* the actual birth of Christ (Matthew 2:1-12). They followed the star that gave light heralding the One who brings light to people (see Isaiah 42:6, 49:6; Luke 2:32; John 1:4, 5, 7-9, 8:12; Acts 13:47, 26:23).

---

[12] Augustine, quoted in Cullmann, 1956:31.

Other Activities Associated with Christmas

We all know that the commercial world benefits enormously from Christmas. Retail stores usually do their best sales at this time while entertainment centres cater for large crowds. It is a time for merrymaking and the giving of presents. This too has its origins in the merriment of the Roman festival of *Saturnalia* which was also associated with behavioural licence such as excessive drinking, gambling and sexual promiscuity. This has carried over into the modern world where Christmas is a time of merrymaking, money-making and, sadly, misery for the lonely and abused.

The activities of Christmas also have origins in Icelandic and early Anglo-Saxon celebrations. The Yule feast, from whence we get the expression *Yuletide*, also seems to be associated with the 'return' of the sun and good harvests. The mistletoe, common in England, was believed by the Druids to have miraculous powers of healing while the idea of the Christmas tree originated in Germany at the beginning of the 17th century when evergreen branches were used as decorations.

The Santa Claus idea is rooted in various beliefs. One suggests that mythical visitors – good and bad – arrived at different seasons, blending pagan legends with traditional stories about saints. One such winter visitor, known in different countries as Santa Claus, Father Christmas, St. Nicholas, St. Martin, the Weihnachtsmann or Père Noel, came to give varying degrees of reward and punishment to the celebrants. The name St. Nicholas, often associated with Santa Claus, originates from the Bishop of Myra who became well known for this generosity to the poor. He died on December 6th 345, but in the 11th century his bones were moved to Bari in Italy where a cult developed in which members gave gifts to each other on the anniversary of Bishop Nicholas' death. These including the filling of children's stockings with presents, a practice adopted from an earlier cultish practice in the city.

In terms of the Christian celebration, some myths have carried over into today's activities such as in nativity plays. For example, there is no record in the gospels of Mary having ridden on a donkey to Bethlehem (though it is possible, for at least part of the journey). Jesus was not born in a stable as we know it today, but more likely in a cave or grotto which was the common shelter for animals and continues to be so in some local areas. Visitors to Bethlehem may visit the Church of the Nativity which is built over the cave in which Jesus is believed to have been born. It is the oldest church in the Middle East and a World Heritage site. Tourists are also often directed to the Shepherds Fields nearby where a similar cave is on view.

Another surviving myth is that of three kings who brought gifts to Jesus. Consider, for example, the hymn *We three kings of orient are*. The wise men who visited the infant Jesus were known as *magi* who were associated with magic and astrology, amongst other things, and no indication is given of their number. The timing of their visit is also in question. According to the gospel writer Matthew, they visited the infant Jesus in a house where it is unlikely he was born, and therefore suggests some time afterwards.

The narrative of the visit of the magi, the family's escape to Egypt and Herod's subsequent slaughter of all boys in Bethlehem under two years of age is found in Matthew chapter 2:1-18.

Some Theological Reflections

The theological term denoting Christ's entrance into this world as a human baby, the *incarnation*, literally means the act of embodying or 'being made' flesh. This derives from John 1:14, *The Word became flesh and made his dwelling among us.* The hymn writer Charles Wesley summed this up succinctly in the words: *The incarnate Deity, our God contracted to a span, incomprehensibly made man.*

A key passage which declares this is Philippians 2:5-8:

> …Christ Jesus: Who, being in very nature God, did not consider equality with God something to be used to his own advantage; rather, he made himself nothing by taking the very nature of a servant, being made in human likeness. And being found in appearance as a man, he humbled himself by becoming obedient to death— even death on a cross!

That Jesus was human is demonstrated by the fact that he was hungry and ate food, was tired and had to sleep, expressed the emotions of joy, sorrow and anger, touched people, perspired, bled and died from injury. That he was divine is attested to in numerous passages of scripture, both by himself and by others. This concept of human yet divine is known as the *hypostatic union* i.e. how God the Son, Jesus Christ, took on a human nature, yet remained fully God at the same time; not a 'mix' of humanity and divinity, but a united being without loss of separate identity. Paul, in his letter to the Colossians, describes this quite clearly:

> The Son is the image of the invisible God, the firstborn over all creation. For in him all things were created: things in heaven and on earth, visible and invisible, whether thrones or powers or rulers or authorities; all things have been created through him and for him. He is before all things, and in him all things hold together. (Colossians 1:15-17),

and

> For God was pleased to have all his fullness dwell in him, and through him to reconcile to himself all things, whether things on earth or things in heaven, by making peace through his blood, shed on the cross. (Colossians 1:19-20).

As a result, he is honoured above all things, as the Philippians passage continues:

> Therefore God exalted him to the highest place and gave him the name that is above every name, that at the name of Jesus every knee should bow, in heaven and on earth and under the earth, and every tongue acknowledge that Jesus Christ is Lord, to the glory of God the Father.
> (Philippians 2: 9-11)

Describing the incarnation, the early church father, St. Augustine, put it succinctly:

> He by whom all things were made was made one of all things. The Son of God by the Father without a mother became the Son of man by a mother without a father. The Word Who is God before all time became flesh at the appointed time (St. Augustine, Sermon 187) … holding fast His own divinity, He became partaker of our infirmity, that we, being changed into some better thing, might, by participating in His righteousness and immortality, lose our own properties of sin and mortality, and preserve whatever good quality He had implanted in our nature perfected now by sharing in the goodness of His nature. For as by the sin of one man we have fallen into a misery so deplorable, so by the righteousness of one Man, who also is God, shall we come to a blessedness inconceivably exalted. (St. Augustine, City of God, xxi, 15).

He went on to say:

> Man's maker was made man,
> that He, Ruler of the stars, might nurse at His mother's breast;
> that the Bread might hunger, the Fountain thirst,
> the Light sleep,
> the Way be tired on its journey;
> that the Truth might be accused of false witness, the Teacher be beaten with whips,
> the Foundation be suspended on wood; that Strength might grow weak;
> that the Healer might be wounded; that Life might die.
> (Augustine of Hippo, Sermons 191.1)

Fowler (1998) argues for the incarnation as follows:

> Christmas can only be understood theologically as the singular divine event that it was if we recognize that the eternal and infinite God intervened and took action to intersect with man in space/time human history in order to invest Himself in a human creature for the purpose of assuming the consequences of sin and restoring humanity to its divinely intended function. The God of the universe voluntarily took the initiative of acting in His grace to condescend and "come down from heaven".

He refers to the third chapter of the Gospel of John to support this.

The German theologian Helmut Thielicke speaks about Christ as "stamped from the beginning by a unique mode of being, namely, by the fact that in him the Eternal Word became flesh and came into our history"[13].

It is clear that the central purpose of Christ's coming was to win back humankind from sin by his vicarious death on the cross. This is summed up in the well-known verse from John's Gospel, 3:16:

> For God so loved the world that he gave his one and only Son, that whoever believes in him shall not perish but have eternal life.

While the incarnation is a foundational belief of the Christian Church, the celebratory event of 25th December is somewhat controversial and brings some divisions amongst Christians.

There is no record in the New Testament that the early church celebrated Christ's birth. Jesus told His disciples to remember His death by partaking in the Lord's Supper or Holy Communion (see Luke 22:14-20) but said nothing about remembering His birthday.

---

[13] Thielicke, 1965.

The Apostle Paul therefore taught about the former (see 1 Corinthians 11:17-24) but said nothing about the latter.

This brings us to the problem of *syncretism*. The theologian Schreiter suggests the term derives from "the study of the religious ferment in the Mediterranean Basin at the beginning of the Common Era when competing cults borrowed heavily from one another and were constantly reshaping themselves into new forms"[14]. Theologians such as Schreiter and Luzbetak argue that Christianity itself has been influenced from 'outside' by cultures in which it has lived, including vestiges from early Old Testament times. In other words, as God's revelation to humankind has developed, the various cultures of the times have coloured both the worldview and the god-view of the people and thus the record of scripture. Schreiter also speaks about the social activities of popular religion which involve celebrations that include feast days for anniversaries of miraculous events and certain seasonal events such as harvest celebrations. Elements of, and events in, nature can also provide cause for celebration and feasting as we have seen above. These can gradually change and be 'mixed' over the passage of time as new inputs are applied. Cullmann describes Constantine as "not so much a Christian as a conscious syncretist: he strove after a synthesis of Christianity and the valuable elements of paganism".

True syncretism, however defined, is seen by some as a theologically untenable amalgam of beliefs and/or practices which alter the tenet of the original. This happened in Old Testament times when the people of Israel allowed themselves to come under the influence of Baal worship and other foreign religious practices, thus incurring God's anger. The Bible is clear about the jealousy of God. The many challenges to holiness in scripture serve to call people to return from compromise and unfaithfulness to the God of their creation and redemption. While traditionally this has been easier in the western Christianized countries, it is increasingly more difficult in the highly secularised modern day and still poses a problem in

---

[14] Schreiter, 1985.

mission fields of the developing world where numerous cultures traversing many centuries are encountered.

Schreiter distinguishes between three types of syncretism: (1) where Christianity and other traditions come together and amalgamate with the other traditions(s) providing the framework; (2) where, by means of a similar combination, Christianity forms the basic framework; and (3) where only selected aspects of Christianity are incorporated into a cultural tradition.

The Christmas celebratory event seems to fit best into Schreiter's first category and its development has certainly served to enhance the witness and profile of the Christian faith as it proclaims the appearing of the Christ child.

However the pagan origins of Christmas may concern us, it has nonetheless been the persuasion of many great Christian people through history that the Christ-birth event should be celebrated, both as an act against parallel pagan festivals and in spite of them. Cullmann argues that Christmas must be seen in the light of Good Friday and Easter; that Christ is at one and the same time the redeemer of mankind and of all creation and therefore pivotal to God's identification with humankind and our responsive worship; and that Christmas should be symbolically associated with nature since Christ, the creator of all things, brought light to the world and "the whole creation...made to refer to Christ...looks for its redemption in him (Schreiter)". Similarly, Thielicke (1965) argues that the fact that God the Father who loves the world and created it demonstrates his love for 'me' in such a way that he sent his Son to be light and life and peace and gave himself for 'me', is the reason why he holds the festival dear. Referring to the Christmas celebration he says, "I join with the shepherds and the wise men from the East in adoring the miracle of Bethlehem. And if I am unsure about the "whether" and the "how" of the sign, I nevertheless look to him to whom the sign points, "The eternal Father's only Son," as Luther's Christmas hymn says. I look to the "new sunshine" that comes from the "eternal light," and I worship him "whom the world could not inwrap" and now "lies in Mary's lap." So why should I not say with joy the words "born of the Virgin Mary," and why should there be any point at all where I could not join the chorus of the Christmas hymns?"

The German theologian Moltmann argues that the Christmas event is demonstrative of God's clear love and identification with humankind, in particular the poor and oppressed, and calls for us to do the same (Moltmann, 1983).

Of course, it is possible to take the radically opposed view that, since Christmas has pagan roots, there is no way that a Christian can participate in the event. Argument for this is usually based in the strong warnings that occur in the Old Testament against any form of compromise with other gods and the practices of surrounding cultures associated with those gods, and similar warnings in the New Testament about various forms of syncretism and unholy compromises (for example in Paul's letters to the Corinthians, Galatians and Colossians, and John in The Revelation). Counter arguments would view this as a somewhat truncated approach which sees only the origins and not the subsequent 'sanctified' developments of the celebration.

Conclusion

There are at least three positions we can take regarding Christmas:

(a) We can write off the whole idea of such a celebration as the continuation of a pagan event and refuse to participate in any church related or even community related festivities. This is the standpoint taken by the sectarian Jehovah's Witnesses and some Christian groups.

(b) We can accept the December 25th date as originally pagan but identify with a number of early Christians and theologians through the centuries in proclaiming a Christian perspective or standard on the event, thus challenging or overriding any pagan associations. We would then be descendants of those who Christianized the pagan practices of the past.

(c) We can ignore the origins of the Christmas festival but still celebrate the Christ birth event on a date of our own choosing thereby declaring a 'pure' celebration of the 'beginning' of the incarnation.

Whatever our position, we must not forget that the festival we know as Christmas has a distinctly northern hemispheric origin and is therefore somewhat irrelevant for people in the southern hemisphere in terms of the *context* of the celebration. Their winter solstice is six months later and therefore the familiar things such as snow and some other features associated with traditional Christmas celebrations are not present. Linked to this is the fact that all of the calculations people have used over the centuries to try and arrive at a date for Jesus' birth are irrelevant since there is no sound basis for such.

Many Christians would not be opposed to people who choose not to celebrate Christmas for sincere reasons, but most have no problem in celebrating it themselves. Their position would be that if God is the God of creation (Genesis 1.1; Psalm 8; John 1:1, etc.) and Jesus the one who has ultimate supremacy – Lord of all creation and the one in whom all things hold together (Colossians 1:15*ff*) – then we are able to worship him on December 25th. One cannot easily ignore all the rich hymnology, prose and poetry of advent written in adoration and praise of him who came to redeem lost humanity and offer peace, love and hope to all by his life, death and resurrection. His appearing is indeed marvellous, albeit not correctly marked in time. He is Lord over against any pagan activities and those whose wills are surrendered to him have little to fear. The need is to tell the world the good news.

POST SCRIPT

SOME QUESTIONS TO PONDER

1. What would be the consequences for the church, Christian witness and the world in general if there was no Christmas celebration?

2. Do you deem the fact that the Christmas celebratory event has its origin in a pagan festival provides a possible inroad for evil? If so, does the Christian emphasis on December 25th banish such evil and/or does the seemingly pagan way in which Christmas is celebrated by so many confirm the malaise?

3. If God is Sovereign Lord of the universe (i.e. over all creation) and the one who loved the world so much that he gave his only Son for the salvation of humankind, how do you believe he looks upon sincere Christian celebrations of the birth of his Son, even if it is on 25th December? And what are we to make of all the inspired writings and hymnology that have arisen out of the Christmas event? Is it irrelevant?

4. How would you compare Christmas with the Easter celebration? Is it more or less important?

5. Do you believe that you can have a relationship with God in Christ? In this regard it is recommended you read the

first, third, eighth and 14th chapters of John's gospel in the New Testament part of the Bible.

Furthermore, the Christmas message is forceful in its call for peace and goodwill to all people and traditionally a time of extra care and concern for the poor and needy. Does that resonate with you?

CHAPTER 3

WHAT CHRISTMAS MEANS TO ME AND HOW WE CELEBRATE IT: THE TESTIMONIES OF PEOPLE AROUND THE WORLD

Anna Nystad (Norway)

I find myself caught between love and gratitude for Christmas and a certain annoyance about the Christmas season.

The reason for the season is to celebrate the greatest gift that has been given to us – Jesus, the Son of God. We give gifts to each other to celebrate His birthday, a symbol of the greatest gift of life.

I love the fact that we have a time to celebrate the immense love of God together with church, family and friends. However, there is a great deal of distraction around the season: all the relatives we *have* to visit, the decorations we *have* to put up, the gifts we *have* to buy. What is it we are really celebrating? Is it about Jesus, family bonds and loved ones, or has it become a celebration of possessions and "stuff"? Judging by the commercial successes of the season it seems that "stuff" is the main focus. Unless I distance myself from society's hype around Christmas, I struggle every year to not make it about *me*: what *I* want under the Christmas tree and what gifts *I* want to give to others. My focus gets diverted onto "stuff" instead of having my focus on God with gratitude for what He has done for us in Jesus and for what I have – both materially and relationally.

Christmas in Norway is celebrated on the eve of December 25th. The morning is full of preparations for the big feast. Around noon the church bells chime to call in the first of two Christmas services. Shops close and families dressed in the traditional costume (*Bunad*) or other formal wear make their way to the state church. After church the feast commences, followed by a visit from *Jule Nissen* (Santa Claus) and gifts are opened. Between the 24th and New Year shops are open for only a short period on certain days; it's time off work to be spent with the family.

I live in a little town in Norway and I love the aesthetics of the Norwegian traditions during Christmas. It's cold, dark and snowy, so the decorations consist mainly of lights: fairy lights in the trees outside and a big star in the window to symbolise the star that led the worshippers to baby Jesus. It's all very quaint and cosy.

Anna Nystad lives in Nottoden, Norway. She is married to Carl-Magnus and they have a family of three. They are involved in a Norwegian Mission Church.

Chris Chinaire (Zimbabwe)

The best Christmas memories I have are from my childhood in Zimbabwe, previously Rhodesia. Though Christmas falls right in the middle of the rainy season, we rarely had showers on Christmas day. Every year, three generations came together at the family homestead in Shangure, Goromonzi. The theme was family, sharing and togetherness, and everyone made a point of being there.

The homestead, at the foot of a large mountain, was a 10 acre plot of fertile red soil. My grandparents grew cotton, groundnuts, sweet potatoes, pumpkins, maize and other crops. Around Christmas time, the maize was a uniformly waist high, a rich military green promising a bumper harvest. The orchard was buzzing with bees attracted to overripe peaches and discarded mango stones.

The whole family would arrive by Christmas Eve and we would share the evening meal together in the large round kitchen hut where we spent most of the evenings. The meal was cooked on an open fire and dished out to be shared among groups of four or five. The rest of the evening was spent updating the family of each other's triumphs and challenges, and we took cultural trips down the family tree where I learned about my ancestral roots and committed to memory the names of my great grandfathers.

By the end of the day the sky looked like a giant black velvet canvas with sprinkled with millions of twinkling stars. Thousands of crickets in the undergrowth led the sounds of the night orchestra. My brothers, cousins and I slept on reed mats in a large room, the excitement of being among family and the expectancy of Christmas rendering the thick darkness less daunting.

Tiny rays of the sun from the distant horizon in the east heralded the beginning of a typical Christmas morning. Roosters flapped their wings and let out cries of jubilation while doves cooed from hidden branches in trees. My grandmother, Ambuya, was among the first to rise and always made the fire in the kitchen hut to symbolise that the home fire would burn as long as she lived.

On rising, my brothers, cousins and I would extend morning greetings to everyone older than us, fetch water from the well, bring firewood to the kitchen and make ourselves available for any task like feeding the chickens and gathering eggs under the close supervision of my grandfather.

After washing and dressing up in new clothes bought for the occasion, we would join the whole family for breakfast in the warmth of the sun. Together we would devour a few loaves of bread to kick start a day of relentless feasting that saw gaps between meals almost disappear. Once the sun was overhead a large leafy tree nearby provided both shelter from the heat and a congregating point for the whole family. Home brewed beer, prepared for over a week by Ambuya and my aunts was made available for the men. An assortment of lukewarm soft drinks provided a wide choice for the rest of us. For lunch we had rice and fried chicken in onion and tomato sauce.

As they reminisced on times gone by and updated us on recent events, my father and his siblings would in turn express their gratitude for the opportunity to come together as a family. However, despite wise counsel from family members to cherish these times, my cousins, brothers and I tended to take them for granted and only decades later came to fully appreciate the special things we did together at Christmas with our grandparents, long since gone.

Now Christmas is no longer just a family gathering for me. It is a global celebration of the miraculous physical birth of the Saviour of the world, Jesus Christ. The purpose of Christ's life on earth is the climax of the greatest love story of all time. I celebrate an internal peace that was brought about by His perfect justice, embrace the freedom that He came to secure for us and am reminded that for love's sake, my Heavenly Father gave all for my soul.

Chris Chinaire was raised and educated in Harare, Zimbabwe. He moved to England in 1999 with his wife Tembi and son, Ruvheneko. Chris has worked as a Business Intelligence professional for an international law firm in London and has served on the leadership of two city churches.

Darrell Davidson (England)

For me Christmas is a kaleidoscope of memories and the promise for the future. As a young child, what excited me was the evocative smell of the Christmas tree, its twinkling lights, the presents beneath and the promise of a special day. However, seldom did the day live up to expectations since it was often fraught with tension. This usually focussed on the preparation of the Christmas dinner. My mother would be busy cutting up the sprouts and potatoes while Dad was simultaneously preparing an enormous fried breakfast – a perfect recipe for family angst! For us there was no visit to church – just the hollow feeling left after the presents were opened.

My father was a musician and Christmas often revolved around seasonal concerts. As a boy, Christmas for me started with the Service of Nine Carols and readings at the Royal Overseas League in London which Dad conducted. I loved the carols and the story of the nativity;

there was a gentle naivety about the occasion which touched me deeply.

When I was a teenager my father produced a recording of Handel's Messiah which I loved – and still do. This gave me a strong sense that there was so much more to Christmas than the rampant commercialism I saw all around me.

As a young married man, I thoroughly enjoyed the familial bonding and fun shared during Christmas visits to my wife's extended family. Besides that, seeing Christmas through my daughters' eyes was a great experience – all the excitement and anticipation of the day with little of the tension and disappointment experienced as a boy.

My first visit to my wife's Baptist church at Christmas gave me a new perspective of how church could be. There was a friendly atmosphere full of people who were fun to be with. This started a journey which led to my wife's baptism and me becoming a Christian.

Now Advent and Christmas mean a great deal to me. On one occasion when asked to help out at a Christmas service I created an eight foot high advent card. Once we had opened out the various windows I removed it from its support structure – a rough old wooden cross. Christmas and Easter are irrevocably entwined for me, with Christmas being a wonderful promise of what Jesus did for us on the cross at Easter.

Darrell Davison is a conductor, cellist and composer who lives in South London with his wife Elizabeth, a fellow musician. They have two married daughters and four grandchildren.

Deborah Lyons (USA)

One of my happiest memories of Christmas includes a summer picnic, a sweaty Santa in a thin cotton suit and a gaggle of friends chasing him around the lawn for the expected presents. This was in South Africa where Christmas comes in the summer and the thought of "chestnuts roasting on an open fire" seems rather unappealing. Many traditions such as dressing up a willing bearded man in a red suit, though geographically out of sync, persisted. Tinsel icicles and spray-on-frost for the tree come to mind. As a child I simply enjoyed chasing Father Christmas and didn't stop to consider the humour of it.

As I grew older and moved to the Northern hemisphere, I experienced real snowfall at Christmas time. The songs about a winter wonderland seemed more fitting. Still, in a Western tradition, there always seems to be something of the ridiculous perpetuated at Christmas. In California, Christmas advertising starts early with specials being announced as soon as October. The season has become a riot of consumerism and corporatizing of traditions completely disconnected from their source. I have never quite felt comfortable with the majority of songs played on the radio (starting punctually the day after Thanksgiving) such as Burt Ives' "A Holly Jolly Christmas". These songs are cheery and fun and have been part of the tradition of Christmas for so long that they themselves conjure up feelings of excitement. But to stop there, or to get lost in the sea of shopping, is to entirely miss its meaning.

As a college student I would attend the Christmas services in our campus chapel. There was always a candlelit service where the minister, Dr. McGonigal, would tell the story of the Messiah's birth, lighting a candle as each character entered the scene: a candle for Mary and one for Joseph; one for the newborn child; more candles for the angels and the shepherds and three candles for the wise men. As he continued to tell the story and the characters exited, he would put out the candles one by one until there was only a single one left burning – that which represented the Christ-child. We would then sit in silence in a darkened sanctuary, keenly focused on the light of that one small candle and realizing that all the darkness in the room could not quench it. Then Dr. McGonigal would invite each one of us to come and light a candle we had been given. After a few minutes of people shuffling past the single candle at the front, the room was brilliant with the glow of a hundred candles. We could see one another's faces. All that light had come from one small candle. After singing a carol, we would walk out into the cold snowfall, carrying our lighted candles and slowly dispersing on our separate ways home.

This is one of my most cherished Christmas memories. Instead of a shopping extravaganza or a walk down a 1950's soundtrack,

Christmas became a solemn and beautiful reminder of how Christ enters our lives, bringing joy and giving us his light to spread into the world.

Deborah Lyons lives in central California with her husband, James, and their three children. Most of her formative years were spent in South Africa and the USA, but she has also lived in England and India. Deborah is a college English instructor and attends a Mennonite Brethren Church.

Victor Nazareth (India)

In India Christmas is known as *Bada Din* (literally 'Big Day'). The name – originating in North India – puzzled me at first and I thought that it simply referred to Christmas as the big day when Jesus was born. I later discovered that the name referred to the Winter Solstice, marking the time of year when the day starts getting longer ('bigger'). Anyway, the two events are linked and many know that it is also marks Christmas or the birth of Christ.

With India opening up its economy to the West over 30 years ago, Christmas became more commercialized. Now the celebration is not just linked to churches and the minority Christian population but also to the trappings of Christmas – trees, Santas, sweets and shopping for presents. Suddenly Christmas was being celebrated by all.

There was a time when our conservative Christian family did not believe that Jesus was born on 25th December – and for good historic reasons – so we did not decorate our home with trees and lights. One Christmas we found our young son taking one of the indoor potted plants and decorating it like a Christmas tree and placing his toy cars below it as gifts. Our hearts relented and we gave into Christmas decorations and celebrations. Our son had seen our Hindu neighbours decorating their homes for Christmas and, in his own way, was doing ours.

Cities are where it is most common to see folk of all backgrounds celebrate Christmas with Santa hats, house decorations, lights and party celebrations. Our nation's practice of giving public holidays to all communities means that Christians get two holidays in the year:

Good Friday and Christmas. This helps put an increased focus on the day. People of all faiths flock to churches for midnight services and to shopping malls for the fun and frolic.

Since Christmas in India draws the attention of the nation to the birth of Christ, it is the best time of the year to share the good news of the purpose of Christ's incarnation. Many Christians use this as the prime season for preaching the gospel. It's one time in the year when even the hardest opponents of the faith are unlikely to desist. We have used this occasion to sing carols in malls and in the homes of our neighbours. We have often been invited by the community centres to hold open Christmas services for the entire community. It has been a great blessing to share our worship of Jesus with all in our city.

Victor Nazareth and his wife Esther are pioneer church planters in the National Capital Region of India and oversee New Life Churches in the area. Parents of three adult children, they are passionate about sharing the good news with people and have and many spiritual children. Victor has a PhD in Engineering from the USA but left that field of employment more than 30 years ago to serve in Christian ministry.

Ramona Stevens (Philippines)

The Philippines is the only country in Asia with a majority Christian population. Filipinos formally commence the celebration of the Christmas season by attending the first of nine "misa de gallo" (pre-dawn or early morning masses) on 16 December. I have lovely memories of this tradition – waking up at four o'clock in the morning and looking forward to buying various traditional Filipino cakes and sweets – made from rice – from the stall outside the church building after each mass.

The "misa de gallo" ends on the evening of 24 December. After mass all my family would return home and eat the "noche buena" (Christmas eve dinner) together.

First thing on Christmas morning we would excitedly open the Christmas presents we believed Santa Claus had brought us for being good. Filipinos are very family-oriented and hospitable so Christmas day is always the best time for family and relatives to get together and share the extravagantly prepared traditional meal. This is also the most important time for us catch up with each other's' lives.

I was brought up in the Roman Catholic faith and taught that Christmas is the celebration of the birth of the Son of God who was born on the 25th of December with the mission of saving people from their sins. It is evident from the history of the Philippines that we celebrate Christmas for the longest period. The Christmas atmosphere starts as early as September when the "ber" months are ushered in. This refers to the last four months of the year. Christmas celebrations finally end on the Epiphany, commemorating the visit of the Magi to the child Jesus.

It is a common practice for many Filipinos to decorate their houses with the traditional Filipino adornments such as a colourful "parol" (star shaped lantern) on the door or window of their houses. Public and private offices also share this tradition.

There are really only two seasons in the Philippines: wet (June to October) and dry (April and May). December is considered the coolest month in the Philippines but not cold enough for snow. Still, Christmas trees and nativity scenes are common sight everywhere.

Christmas carolling is another important Filipino tradition. At a young age, I loved going out with the carollers and joined in the singing from house to house, thus spreading the spirit of Christmas. Another purpose of this practice is to raise money for good causes during the festive season.

Christmas has a far deeper meaning for me now since receiving Jesus as my Saviour and Lord. I find Christmas celebrations in England quieter and would love to go back home at Christmas to re-live some of what I used to know in my childhood – sadly missed for many years.

Ramona Stevens resides in the south of England with her English husband and their son. She is a registered nurse working at a local hospital and attends a multicultural evangelical church.

BIBLIOGRAPHY

CULLMANN, O. 1956. *The Early Church: Historical and Theological Studies*. London: SCM Press.

FOWLER, JAMES A. 1998. Christmas Considered Theologically. http://www.christinyou.net/christmas/xmastheology.html

LUZBETAK, L.J. 1988. *The church and cultures*. Maryknoll: Orbis.

MCCARTHUR, John. 20 December 2009. The theology of Christmas. http://www.gty.org/resources/sermons/80-354

MOLTMANN, J. 1983. *The Power of the Powerless* London: SCM Press.

SCHREITER, R.J. 1985. *Constructing local theologies*. London: SCM Press.

THIELICKE, Helmut. 1965. *Between Heaven and Earth: Conversations with American Christians*. Translated and edited by John W. Doberstein. Westport, CT: Greenwood, 1975, 1965.

THE WORLD BOOK ENCYCLOPEDIA. 1990. Chicago: World Book Inc.

TRUE JESUS CHURCH: http://www.tjc.org/showArticle.aspx?aid=7219

WESLEY, CHARLES. 1707-1799. Let heaven and earth combine.

APPENDIX

OLD TESTAMENT PROPHECIES SPECIFICALLY ABOUT THE BIRTH AND INFANT YEARS OF CHRIST

Born of a virgin

Isaiah 7:14

Therefore the Lord himself will give you a sign: The virgin will conceive and will give birth to a son, and will call him Immanuel.

...of kingly lineage

Isaiah 9:6-7

For to us a child is born, to us a son is given, and the government will be on his shoulders. And he will be called Wonderful Counsellor, Mighty God, Everlasting Father, Prince of Peace. Of the increase of his government and peace there will be no end. He will reign on David's throne and over his kingdom, establishing and upholding it with justice and righteousness from that time on and forever. The zeal of the LORD Almighty will accomplish this.

...in Bethlehem

Micah 5:2

But you, Bethlehem Ephrathah, though you are small among the clans of Judah, out of you will come for me one who will be ruler over Israel, whose origins are from of old, from ancient times.

Worshipped and gifted by kings

Psalm 72:10

May the kings of Tarshish and of distant shores bring tribute to him. May the kings of Sheba and Seba present him with gifts.

Isaiah 60:3,6b

Nations will come to your light, and kings to the brightness of your dawn.

And all from Sheba will come, bearing gold and incense and proclaiming the praise of the Lord.

Taken to, and returned from, Egypt

Hosea 11:1

When Israel was a child, I loved him, and out of Egypt I called my son.

Infants slaughtered

Jeremiah 31:15

This is what the LORD says: "A voice is heard in Ramah, mourning and great weeping, Rachel weeping

APPENDIX

OLD TESTAMENT PROPHECIES SPECIFICALLY ABOUT THE BIRTH AND INFANT YEARS OF CHRIST

Born of a virgin

Isaiah 7:14

Therefore the Lord himself will give you a sign: The virgin will conceive and will give birth to a son, and will call him Immanuel.

...of kingly lineage

Isaiah 9:6-7

For to us a child is born, to us a son is given, and the government will be on his shoulders. And he will be called Wonderful Counsellor, Mighty God, Everlasting Father, Prince of Peace. Of the increase of his government and peace there will be no end. He will reign on David's throne and over his kingdom, establishing and upholding it with justice and righteousness from that time on and forever. The zeal of the LORD Almighty will accomplish this.

...in Bethlehem

Micah 5:2

But you, Bethlehem Ephrathah, though you are small among the clans of Judah, out of you will come for me one who will be ruler over Israel, whose origins are from of old, from ancient times.

Worshipped and gifted by kings

Psalm 72:10

May the kings of Tarshish and of distant shores bring tribute to him. May the kings of Sheba and Seba present him with gifts.

Isaiah 60:3,6b

Nations will come to your light, and kings to the brightness of your dawn.

And all from Sheba will come, bearing gold and incense and proclaiming the praise of the Lord.

Taken to, and returned from, Egypt

Hosea 11:1

When Israel was a child, I loved him, and out of Egypt I called my son.

Infants slaughtered

Jeremiah 31:15

This is what the LORD says: "A voice is heard in Ramah, mourning and great weeping, Rachel weeping for her children and refusing to be comforted, because her children are no more."

Presented in the temple

Malachi 3:1

"I will send my messenger, who will prepare the way before me. Then suddenly the Lord you are seeking will come to his temple; the messenger of the covenant, whom you desire, will come," says the Lord Almighty.[1]

---

[1] *This may also encompass Jesus' entering the temple as recorded in Matthew 21, Mark 11 and John 2.*